The Language of Life in Seconds

Also by Jennifer D. Maree

Blending Cultures: A Settling Story
Medicine, Music and Mirth
Blending Cultures: A Moving Story
Ubuntu: The Spirit of African Transformation Management (co-author)
Fifty Fabulous Facts for First Time Corporate Facilitators

Jennifer D. Maree

The Language of Life in Seconds

Acknowledgements

I would like to thank Doreen Clarke for constant encouragement and support and Leon for proofreading and inspiration.

I also want to thanks those who provided comment on the work:
Susan, Nicola, Thomas, Chris, Maya, Vijaya, Betty, Greg, Josie, Liz, Nick, Robert, Blondie, Margaret, Jax, Erica, and Lenore.

You helped it all become a reality.

To Doreen

The Language of Life in Seconds
ISBN 978 1 74027 827 0
Copyright © Jennifer D. Maree 2013

First published 2013
Reprinted 2015

Ginninderra Press
PO Box 3461 Port Adelaide SA 5015
www.ginninderrapress.com.au

Contents

Exercises at writing groups	7
Your Sacred Place	9
Christmas Invitation	10
My Favourite Memories of Christmas	11
Words and meaning	12
Men at work	13
Life	14
Nature	15
Skies in the Barossa	17
Bowral Garden	18
View from the window	19
The Tree	20
The Fleurieu	21
Clouds	22
Coonawarra to Mt Gambier	23
The Chameleons	24
Hippo 2	25
Landscapes	26
Travelling	27
Suzhou Part IV	29
Suzhou Residential	30
Shanghai	31
Suzhou to Shanghai	32
Visitors at Great Lakes Entertainment	33
Brighton Café	34
Singapore	35
Sacred Seawater	36
For Radia's birthday	37
Serena	38

New York	39
Culture Shock	40
Family	**41**
Mother's sayings	43
Mother's Day	44
Maternal Memoir	45
War Child	46
Adrenoleukodystrophy	47
Bea	48

Exercises at writing groups

Your Sacred Place

You may think it's in the flowers
Or even a shed
You may think it's where the dog cowers
Or lying in bed

You're mistaken if you think it is t'ai chi
Or Pilates
It's not anything beachy
Or mixing with the arties

It's in the mind
A mantra and any location
It's quietness of a different kind
It's meditation

Christmas Invitation

Your presence please
No presents
The invitation
Tim indifferent
Busy
Fixing something as usual
Preoccupied with the tangible
The controllable
The mechanical
Me thinking of the spirit of Christmas
Gone
I love wrapping paper
Ribbons
Christmas labels
The thrill of giving
The joy of receiving
They weren't doing me any favours.

My Favourite Memories of Christmas

Picnics on the beach
Ham, pickles and rye bread
Kicking sand at my siblings
Surfing in on a wave
Showering out all the sand
Before getting into the family car
Kissing all the relatives after a hearty lunch
My brothers were not so keen
Relatives came in many packages
Some colourful
Telling outrageous stories
Some generous
Money in envelopes
Some recycle gifts
The box is most telling
Some are boastful
Constantly telling you how much better
Your cousins are doing
Others are sleigh riders
Cruising through the sky
Like Father Christmas

Words and meaning

Scale
A small shock
A large tree
You weighing everything up
Playing devil's advocate
Trying to pin me down
Measuring everything
Asking me questions I can't answer
How much?
How many?
When?
I remember big picture
Sadness and expectations and desire
Ideas and concepts
Peace and war
Details of the physical world
How her jaw dropped
When her friend described
Her child's school experiences
How his brows furrowed
When he saw the dress she was wearing
The old lady's cheeks curling into dimples
As she watched the child eat the ice cream
Small talk inane to some
Life bread to another

Men at work

Bumblebees commune on flowers
Leaning forward
Arm holding tight
They chew the fat
Caterpillars looking up
Beseechingly looking for commodities
Upsized, downsized, restructured
The outcome is change
Do something
Move in a direction
Look busy
Talk about your hundreds of emails
Commune
Feel better
Collaborate
Call it teamwork
Goals agreed
Time to go

Life

It's not a war just a battle
It's not a marathon just a race
Trite sayings that minimise transitions
Trivialise success and failure
Deal with triumph and loss
As if they are the same
With recipe remedies
Rolling them out
Big and thick
What doesn't kill us makes us stronger
What you sow shall you reap
Listen to us
Hear us
Absorb

Nature

Skies in the Barossa

Sun leaning languidly
Golden on arm
Green leaves crawling through empty angrily embalm
Trunks sprouting anew

Rain has come
Promised often, not delivered
Coats needed while we quivered
A messiah's work is done

Gratitude all round
Lawns in full regalia
This is the true Australia
Flowers abound

I love the rain
Also enjoy warmth and sun
Awful when we get none
No one to blame

Bowral Garden

The butcher bird
Lauding it over the garden furniture
Standing regally
On the latticed metal chair
A proprietary stare
Total ownership
I tap the window
Consumer of small birds
Please go away
Defensively
He looks at me
A 'how dare you' look
I walk outside
Gone

View from the window

I see you peering into my window
Your view of me
I loom large
You are so tiny
Perfectly beautiful
Indigenous colours
Bright green, purple and red
I am in red man-made plastic
You are so fragile
I can take care of myself
Anyone can pick you
Cut you out
Drown you in a vase
Keep you imprisoned
Throw you in a bin

The Tree

You have seen so much
Helped so many birds
Protected countless people
Towering over us
Watching us
Sheltering the universe
Preserving knowledge
Discreetly
I hear your whispers
I wish I spoke your language
The breeze clears
Your branches extend
Giving us promise
We will go on

The Fleurieu

Rubensesque landscape beckons
All milky thighs
Curvaceous posteriors
Then a sign clean skin wines
Consumerism calls
Better to look at the Botticelli angels ahead
Turquoise blue
As thighs dress
And reach for the sea
The green tufts
While she covers reaching for more clothing
The sky above
Welcoming the angels
The vines providing a soft bed
In neat rows
So she finds her way

Clouds

The clouds out there are a whole world
Only they measure their inhabitants in weight
To be a heavyweight is to be in exile
Not for that world
An outsider
Lost without trying
Automatic selection
Creating more refugees
For other worlds
Heavy newcomers
With extra baggage
Looking for another place to be

Nature would decide when the clouds could no longer cope
Giving them a chance to unburden
Perhaps just after storms or a light rain
When clouds are empty
Resting
Giving the sun a turn

Coonawarra to Mt Gambier

Coonawarra
Australia's other red centre
Yellow trees
Jamieson's Run
Redman's
Katnook
Penola
Catholic saints
Mary had a little lamb
She also had a saint
Rain, rain go away
Come back another day
I want to explore
See the tornado
Taste wine

The Chameleons

All crossing the road
One side of the body moving
Then the bounce
Other half moving
Rocking to the other side
Almost on walkers
Slow
Laborious
Old before their time
Sometimes green
Sometimes speckled
Ignoring the bitumen
Reverse defensiveness
So you see them
Don't drive over them
Nature thinking

Hippo 2

She is the hippo
Living on salad
Walking in water
Pendulous bosoms
Flabby thighs
Large feet
Big mouth
Droopy cow eyes
She will bite you
Biggest killer in Africa

Landscapes

She scrapes back her hair
Revealing a smoothed face
Helped by tractor marks
A lone diver braves early-morning temperatures
Walkers chat ambling
Runners dodge strollers
Horses dance in the breeze
Bandicoots hide in the bush
Cyclists compete with skateboarders
Space is at a premium
Peace is free
Forty minutes of frenetic pacing
Manly enveloping and inclusive
An old woman's lap
Layers of skirts
Revealing the beach of petticoats

Travelling

Suzhou Part IV

(China)

I want to reflect
Find a quiet place
The garden of the Public Administrator
Peace at last
Sounds of water
Sensual food
Tastes change as you bite
And again as you chew
And again as you swallow
Food lifecycles in the mouth
Sweet, sour, salt
Fragrances hit my nose
I see petals
Falling in front of my eyes
I am alone now
Others present
My mind, a wand to make them disappear
While I meditate
The mantra drowning out smell and taste
Mind juice

Suzhou Residential

(China)

Daytime slippers
Closed bars
Old and new
Clean gardens
Dirty canals
Eastern Venice
Lone bird
Painted trees
Empty traffic towers
Unused remnants
Silent sentries
Cheap pirated DVDs
Directions needed
A chain reaction
All down the street
A crowd gathers
A single pointed finger
The way to go
The Mandarin guide rescues
Sweet nods and smiles
Taxi driver looks at card
A standard at all western hotels
A white seat cover
Dual purpose car
Taxi by day
Transport vehicle by night
Maximum use for optimal rent
Complex
Hidden by a simple surface

Shanghai

(China)

Hybrid
Two
Schizo
Parallel
Ritzy and poor
Viby and dingy
Happy and sad
Bicycle mechanic alongside Porsche
Juxtaposed
Blue singlets and Louis Vuitton
Sweet and sour
Eternity and now
Fast train, hard seats
Waiters serve, soft seats
Stirring needed
Glitzy magazines
Ticket checking
Gate, train, boom
Ticket checking
Open cloakrooms
Internal walls
Ubiquitous trade
Useful scrap
Endless creativity

Suzhou to Shanghai

(China)

Three hundred kilometres per hour
Construction workers in the corner of my eye
24/7 floodlights
Concentration camps of concrete
Battery hen conditions
Soft seats
Hard seats
Class is affordability
Soft seats get you a *Vogue* magazine
Tray service
Personal conductor and extra smiles
Hard seats unimaginable
Better than the view through the windows
Progress

Visitors at Great Lakes Entertainment

(Forster, Australia)

He cradled her
Holding her fragile body
Stroking the lower half
Fingers moving nimbly
Picking
Each sound for his ear only
Then for the audience
Ninety-five per cent original
He said
Lips pressed soothingly on the mike
Foot tapping on a drum
Dung beetles appropriating sand
Bums in the air
Chorus
Thank you for clapping
He said
Nodding in our direction
It usually takes them about an hour
He said
Seamlessly blowing into the mouth organ

Brighton Café

(Adelaide, South Australia)

Mothers-in-law tongue
Green and striped
Provocatively reaching upwards
As if in answer
To the orange lampshades
And brown walls which
Envelop the 1930s house
With creaking wooden floorboards
Which groan with pleasure
As they take the weight of all the
Luxurious cakes the ladies who lunch
Consume and the building of
Friendship as they bond and dine
And reach satiation
Fresh healthy food
Ever-changing staff
Knowing the customers or products is beyond capability
But it is always full
The pings of BlackBerrys
Laptops screening faces

Singapore

I must move in this pattern
My ancestors
Swiss watch mechanists
Clock ticking rhythm
I must move in this process
Uniformity is part of success
The procedure is in my DNA
Standards run through my veins
Consistency makes us stronger
Humidity is irrelevant
Kill it with air conditioning
Always a system
The pendulum of growth

Sacred Seawater

(South Africa)

Every year Triphena collected all the jam and pickle bottles
We took box loads of bottles
To the seaside cottage
Kids taking turns
Filling bottles of seawater
Triphena sold them at a roaring profit
The local witch doctor bought
Countless neighbouring nannies too
Great healer
They said
The stories of the witch doctor
Made us very obedient children
We imagined spells
Far worse than Harry Potter
Once I had food poisoning
Got fed seawater
Vomited my entire stomach
Rapid recovery
Triphena cackled
Told all her friends
Money meant nothing
A week's wages
What did we know?

For Radia's birthday

(South Africa)

Africa is in our blood
Hear the elephants thud
Let us hold hands
Our unity will stop shifting sands
The strength of the lion's roar
Will awaken earth's core
The hippos wallow in the mud
While proteas burst into bud
The baobab tree gives us shade
While many a plan is made
We know how to party and rejoice
Knowing success will result from our choice

Serena

(South Africa)

Long American car pulls up
'Can I have an advance on next week's pay, please?'
One is thinking of the cost of the lift
From her home to our home
And on a Sunday
The driver is dressed very respectably
Probably doing good trade
Usually she works there during the week
While we are up in the big city
She is dressed to the nines
Probably on her way to church
Not limited by pews
The size of the visible
One of brightly coloured cloaks
Tall biblical walking sticks
Walking in a circle
Dancing out in the open
Between trees
And passers-by
Much singing
This is a small village
On a huge dam
The wallet is taken out
Money is given
Little thought of trust or drink
All compassion

New York

(USA)

My friend loves New York
An umbilical cord
A placenta
Centre of her universe
Coffee at Chifley towers
Reminds me of the Big Apple
She said
Yearning pouring out of her voice
Need to visit my sister again
She said
Deep longing oozing from her pores
She loves Israel too
Comes from South Africa
Lives in Sydney
New York is a homeland
She says
Homelands aren't always where you are born
Or where your family is
Or where you die
It's tribal
Spiritual
Colours
Music
How you say hello, laugh, cry
Greet customers
Show love

Culture Shock

I want to see round
A ball
A square
A field
The four poles of AFL
They told me that
ENTJ's love rows and columns
Order
They did not tell me that
This could mean high rises
In grids of grey
Blue trucks in matchbox quantities
Collecting, collecting
Mice running
Cockroaches scurrying
Collecting, collecting
Bits and pieces
Material, metal, glass, bottles
My granny would be so happy
War children saving everything
Frugality
Soap on the windowsill
Sun makes it last longer
Envelopes used back and front
Tearing supermarket bags into strips
Crocheted handbags

Family

Mother's sayings

Waves in the moonlight
Bury me at sea
Symphony concerts
Must see the hands
Followed by crowds
Friends will outlast husbands
Filthy humour
A man is only interested in his stomach and what hangs from it
Legal studies
Fight for women
Play the piano
Be entertaining
Learn useful skills
You can't do ballet when you are old
Dancing on tables
You have to be able to let go
Loyalty
You reap what you sow
Be a Good Samaritan
Help where you can
Ruben women
Who wants an ironing board?
Take your cockroach
Find the humour

Mother's Day

Feathered hands travel over the keyboards
Bouncy jazz to thundering classics
Sunday school hymns to wild parties
Piano towering over Susie Cooper dainties
Persians dwarfing Mozart and Beethoven
Twinset and pearls until brandy and ginger ale
Methodist morals with a cussing mouth
Rhythmic raucous laughter
Erupting as shoes kicked off
The French chef recovering
From the plastic cockroach
In his signature dish
Tournedos of joy

Maternal Memoir

Tender touch
Better than any medicine
Legendary fights
Lifelong friendships
Storyteller
Who never shared her own
Survivor
Who kept drowning
Activist
Who needed one
A girl
Who would have preferred to be a boy
A sufferer
Always helping others with theirs
A revhead
Who needed to go slow

War Child

She was a war child
Born in the thirties
Careful when she dialled
Frugal even in the eighties

Stockings were a special gift
Turned off every light
Chocolate a real lift
Terrified in the night

Never leave food on your plate
Eat every drop
When it's too late
You might have to stop

Adrenoleukodystrophy

A thief came in the night
Stole your sight
Then a burglar came one day
And you didn't know what to say

The doctor came and checked
Then showed you more respect
Said you were dying
Naturally we thought he was lying

We bought jars of special honey
And spent all our money
On medicines and quacks
But still you could not put on your slacks

You were only a child
But death is not mild

Bea

Visiting flowers
Bringing messages of hope
Always positive
Counting blessings
Cooking for everyone
Steak for Fifi
Lemon pudding for Mr Sofianos
Rice dessert for Jerry
Shortbread biscuits for Jenny
White gloves
Regal lashings of love for new tenants
Compassionate landlord
Calling ambulances
Hugging the grieving
Flowers for all occasions
Flowers on the towels
Flowers on the tiles
Flowers on the dresses
Flowers in the flat
Flowers in the window boxes
Flowers in the frames
She saw pollen in everyone
She was a honey

www.ingramcontent.com/pod-product-compliance
Lightning Source LLC
Chambersburg PA
CBHW062206100526
44589CB00014B/1971